THESSALONIKI

21 THINGS TO DO IN 7 DAYS

1. White Tower of Thessaloniki

The White Tower of Thessaloniki is a symbol of the city and one of its most iconic landmarks. Built in the 15th century during the Ottoman period, it served as a fortress, garrison, and prison. Today, it functions as a museum offering insights into Thessaloniki's rich history. Situated on the city's waterfront, the tower provides stunning panoramic views of the Thermaic Gulf from its top level, making it a must-visit for tourists.

Reaching the White Tower is easy. It is centrally located on Nikis Avenue and accessible by public transport, taxi, or on foot if you're exploring the city center. If taking a bus, lines 3, 5, and 6 stop nearby. Walking along the waterfront promenade is another enjoyable way to arrive. Parking is limited, so public transport is recommended.

Tickets cost approximately €8 for adults and €4 for reduced categories, such as students and seniors. Prices may vary slightly depending on the season, so checking ahead is advisable. The tower is open year-round, typically from 8:00 AM to 8:00 PM, but hours may change in winter or during holidays.

Visitors can explore the museum, which spans six floors, each featuring exhibits on the city's history, culture, and daily life over the centuries. Interactive displays and multimedia presentations make the experience engaging. Climbing the spiral staircase to the observation deck is a highlight, offering spectacular views of the city and the sea.

The visit usually takes about 1.5 to 2 hours, depending on how thoroughly you explore the exhibits. It's best to visit in the early morning or late afternoon to avoid crowds, especially during peak tourist season. Comfortable shoes are recommended due to the tower's many stairs.

Don't miss the opportunity to stroll along the waterfront afterward, where you can enjoy cafes, street performers, and a vibrant atmosphere. Combining the White Tower visit with other nearby attractions, such as Aristotelous Square and the Archaeological Museum, makes for a perfect day in Thessaloniki.

2. Aristotelous Square

Aristotelous Square is the heart of Thessaloniki and a vibrant meeting point for locals and tourists alike. Designed by French architect Ernest Hébrard in 1918, it showcases the city's post-fire reconstruction with its grand neoclassical buildings and wide-open space. The square opens up to the Thermaic Gulf, offering beautiful sea views and a bustling atmosphere. It is a hub for cultural events, street performances, and festivals, making it one of the most lively spots in the city. As you stand in the square, you'll notice the symmetry of its architecture, blending Mediterranean charm with European sophistication, creating a perfect backdrop for a leisurely visit.

Getting to Aristotelous Square is simple, as it is centrally located in Thessaloniki's city center. It is easily accessible by public transport, with numerous bus lines stopping nearby, including lines 5, 6, and 33. Walking is another convenient option, especially if you're already exploring the area, as it connects directly to the waterfront promenade and other key attractions. For those driving, parking can be challenging, so public transportation is a better choice. The square is also a starting point for exploring the lively Ladadika District or reaching the nearby Rotunda and Arch of Galerius.

Aristotelous Square is free to visit, making it an ideal stop for travelers on any budget. It is open at all hours, and its dynamic energy changes throughout the day, from the calm morning vibe to the lively evening scene filled with cafes, restaurants, and bars. Visitors can relax at one of the many outdoor terraces, try local delicacies, or enjoy people-watching. Street performers and seasonal markets add to its charm, especially during festivals or the holiday season when the square is beautifully illuminated. For history and architecture enthusiasts, the square's buildings, such as the Electra Palace Hotel, offer a glimpse into Thessaloniki's modern urban planning.

Exploring the square and its surroundings typically takes about 1 to 2 hours, depending on your pace and interest in nearby attractions. It's an excellent starting or ending point for a day of sightseeing, with Aristotelous Street leading directly to the central market areas like Modiano and Kapani. Combining it with a stroll along the waterfront or visits to landmarks like the White Tower ensures a well-rounded Thessaloniki experience. Don't forget your camera, as Aristotelous Square provides some of the most iconic photo opportunities in the city.

3. Ano Poli (Upper Town)

Ano Poli, or the Upper Town, is the most historic and picturesque district of Thessaloniki. Perched on the hillside, it offers a unique blend of traditional Macedonian architecture, narrow cobblestone streets, and stunning panoramic views of the city and the Thermaic Gulf. Unlike the modernized lower city, Ano Poli retains its old-world charm, with colorful houses, historic churches, and remnants of the Byzantine walls and towers that once protected Thessaloniki. This area survived the great fire of 1917, making it a living museum of the city's rich history and culture. Walking through Ano Poli feels like stepping back in time, with every turn offering a glimpse into the city's storied past.

Getting to Ano Poli can be part of the adventure. For those who enjoy walking, the uphill journey from the city center takes about 30 to 40 minutes, with beautiful scenery along the way. If you prefer a more convenient option, public buses like lines 23 and 24 drop you close to the area, making it easily accessible. Taxis are also available and affordable, especially if you're traveling in a group. Once in Ano Poli, walking is the only way to truly explore its narrow streets and hidden gems, so comfortable shoes are a must.

Exploration in Ano Poli is entirely free, though some attractions may have a small fee if you wish to enter. Highlights include the Byzantine Walls, Heptapyrgion Fortress (Yedi Kule), and the Vlatadon Monastery, which offers peaceful gardens and breathtaking views of Thessaloniki. Don't miss the Church of Osios David, known for its stunning mosaics, or the Church of Saint Nicholas Orphanos, a UNESCO World Heritage Site. Strolling through the district, you'll also discover traditional tavernas where you can enjoy authentic Greek cuisine in a serene atmosphere. Local specialties like moussaka and tsipouro pair perfectly with the charm of Ano Poli.

Exploring Ano Poli typically takes about 3 to 5 hours, depending on how many landmarks and tavernas you visit. It's best to visit in the early morning or late afternoon to avoid the midday heat, especially during summer. As the sun sets, the views from the Byzantine Walls or Heptapyrgion Fortress are unforgettable, offering a magical end to your exploration. For photographers, the golden hour lighting adds an extra layer of beauty to this already captivating district.

4. Rotunda of Galerius

The Rotunda of Galerius, one of Thessaloniki's most iconic landmarks, is a massive cylindrical structure built in the early 4th century by Roman Emperor Galerius. Originally intended as a mausoleum or temple, its purpose remains debated among historians. Over time, it was converted into a Christian church, a mosque during the Ottoman period, and now serves as a museum. Its thick, 6-meter walls, combined with its breathtaking mosaics that depict early

Christian artistry, make it an architectural marvel and a UNESCO World Heritage Site. Its towering dome is among the largest of its kind, symbolizing its historical and cultural significance in Thessaloniki's evolving identity.

The Rotunda is located centrally, just a short walk from the Arch of Galerius (Kamara), making it easily accessible on foot. Public transportation options include buses such as lines 3, 5, and 6, which stop nearby, or taxis, which are affordable and convenient given the Rotunda's prominence as a landmark. Its location makes it ideal to combine with visits to nearby attractions, such as the Kamara and Thessaloniki's bustling cafes and shops.

Admission costs approximately €6 for adults, with discounted tickets available for students, seniors, and children, usually priced at €3. It is open throughout the year, typically from 8:00 AM to 8:00 PM, although hours may vary during holidays or winter months, so it's advisable to check in advance. Inside, visitors are greeted with a serene atmosphere that enhances the viewing of its intricate mosaics, including depictions of saints and celestial motifs that highlight the craftsmanship of the era.

A visit to the Rotunda generally takes about an hour, but it can be extended if you immerse yourself in its details. Comfortable footwear is recommended for navigating its uneven floors. Nearby, you'll find charming cafes perfect for enjoying a refreshing break after your visit. Its close proximity to other key landmarks makes the Rotunda a must-visit, offering a tangible connection to Thessaloniki's Roman, Byzantine, and Ottoman past.

5. Arch of Galerius (Kamara)

The Arch of Galerius, also known as Kamara, is one of Thessaloniki's most remarkable ancient monuments, dating back to the early 4th century AD. It was erected by the Roman Emperor Galerius to celebrate his victory over the Persians. The arch is a stunning example of Roman architecture and craftsmanship, with its four massive pillars and intricately carved reliefs depicting scenes of battle and triumph.

Originally part of a grand complex that included the nearby Rotunda, the Kamara still stands as a testament to the power and influence of the Roman Empire in Thessaloniki. Its strategic location, near the city center, makes it a must-visit for anyone interested in the city's Roman past.

Located just a short walk from Aristotelous Square and the Rotunda, the Arch of Galerius is easily accessible. You can reach it on foot by strolling through the vibrant streets of Thessaloniki's city center, or by taking public transport. Bus lines 3, 5, and 6 all pass by the Kamara, and taxis are also a convenient way to get there. Its central location makes it an ideal stop during a day of sightseeing, allowing you to easily explore nearby landmarks such as the White Tower and the Archaeological Museum.

There is no admission fee to visit the Arch of Galerius, as it is an open-air monument, which makes it an excellent option for budget-conscious travelers. It's open to the public at all times, and there is no set visiting schedule, so you can visit whenever you like. The arch's impressive reliefs and architectural grandeur are best appreciated by walking around the monument and observing the intricate details of the carvings. The site typically takes about 30 minutes to explore, but it can be extended if you enjoy taking in the details or capturing photos.

After visiting, you can relax in one of the nearby cafes or continue exploring the bustling streets around the Kamara. With its rich history and central location, the Arch of Galerius provides a fascinating glimpse into Thessaloniki's ancient Roman heritage.

6. Thessaloniki Waterfront (Nea Paralia)

The Thessaloniki Waterfront, or Nea Paralia, is one of the city's most cherished public spaces, offering a blend of natural beauty, cultural attractions, and recreational activities. This scenic promenade stretches along the waterfront, from the White Tower in the west to the new harbor in the east. Nea Paralia has been beautifully redeveloped in recent years, transforming it into a vibrant, pedestrian-friendly area where both locals and tourists can enjoy stunning views of the Thermaic Gulf, the city skyline, and the surrounding mountains. The waterfront is lined with lush green spaces, modern sculptures, and contemporary architecture, offering a peaceful retreat right in the heart of the city.

Getting to the Thessaloniki Waterfront is simple, as it is centrally located along the seafront. The promenade is easily accessible by foot from the city center, making it a perfect destination for a leisurely walk or bike ride. There are also public transportation options such as buses and trams that stop along the waterfront, allowing for easy access from various parts of the city. Taxis are another convenient option, especially if you're coming from farther away.

There is no fee to access Nea Paralia, as it is an open public space. The waterfront is free to explore at all times, making it an excellent choice for tourists on a budget. The area is especially picturesque at sunset when the sky turns vibrant shades of orange and pink, reflecting off the sea. The promenade is equipped with benches and shaded areas, ideal for relaxing while enjoying the views.

While at the waterfront, there are plenty of activities to keep you entertained. You can rent bikes or electric scooters to cruise along the promenade, or take part in one of the many small boat tours that offer views of Thessaloniki from the water. The area is also home to several cafes, bars, and restaurants, where you can sit down and enjoy traditional Greek dishes or fresh seafood. Along the route, you'll encounter several sculptures and monuments, such as the Umbrellas sculpture by Zongolopoulos, and cultural spaces like the Museum of Byzantine Culture and the Thessaloniki Concert Hall.

Exploring the Thessaloniki Waterfront typically takes around 1 to 2 hours, but you could easily spend more time here depending on how much you wish to relax or explore. With its blend of nature, culture, and recreation, Nea Paralia is a perfect place to enjoy the beauty and charm of Thessaloniki.

7. Ladadika District

Ladadika District is one of Thessaloniki's most vibrant and historic neighborhoods, known for its rich cultural heritage, lively atmosphere, and charming architecture. Situated just south of the city's waterfront, Ladadika was once a commercial center, home to the city's oil merchants, and its name comes from the Greek word "ladi" meaning oil. Today, it is a bustling district filled with traditional tavernas, trendy bars, cafes, and a mix of old and new buildings that reflect the city's eclectic character.

The area has undergone significant revitalization in recent years, transforming into a popular destination for locals and tourists alike, especially in the evenings when the streets come alive with music, food, and laughter.

Getting to Ladadika is easy from Thessaloniki's city center. It is located within walking distance from the White Tower, just a few minutes stroll through the central streets. Alternatively, public transportation such as buses or taxis can quickly take you there, as it is well-connected to the rest of the city. The district's central location makes it ideal for combining a visit with other attractions nearby, such as the Archaeological Museum or the Roman Forum.

There is no entrance fee to explore the Ladadika District, as it is an open neighborhood filled with shops and cafes. However, you will want to budget for food, drinks, and any special activities you plan to enjoy. Ladadika is renowned for its dining scene, where you can find authentic Greek meze dishes, seafood, and grilled meats, all served in lively settings. Many of the tavernas feature live music, especially bouzouki performances, which make for a memorable dining experience. The area is also home to several bars and nightclubs, making it a perfect place to enjoy Thessaloniki's nightlife.

A visit to Ladadika typically takes around 2 to 3 hours, but this can easily extend if you decide to stay for dinner or enjoy a drink. The district is perfect for strolling, offering a mix of historical charm and modern energy. Whether you're there for the food, the nightlife, or the lively atmosphere, Ladadika is a must-visit for anyone wanting to experience the heart of Thessaloniki's cultural life.

8. Byzantine Walls

The Byzantine Walls of Thessaloniki are one of the most significant historical landmarks in the city, offering visitors a glimpse into the city's defensive past. These walls were constructed between the 4th and 12th centuries, serving as the main fortifications that protected Thessaloniki from invasions. Stretching for several kilometers, the walls are made up of imposing stone structures, towers, and gates, and are considered one of the most well-preserved examples of Byzantine military architecture in Greece. The walls once encircled the entire city, but much of the structure has been lost over time. Today, portions of the walls remain standing, particularly in the upper town, offering panoramic views of the city below and the surrounding landscapes.

Getting to the Byzantine Walls is relatively easy, especially since the main sections are located near the Ano Poli (Upper Town) area, which is one of the city's most historic and charming neighborhoods. From the city center, you can reach the walls by walking uphill, a journey that takes about 15 to 20 minutes from Aristotelous Square. Alternatively, public buses or taxis can take you to the base of the walls, making it more convenient for those who prefer not to walk. The area around the walls is a peaceful and residential part of Thessaloniki, perfect for exploring at a leisurely pace.

There is no admission fee to visit the Byzantine Walls, as they are open to the public at all times. However, some of the nearby sites, like the Yedi Koule Tower and the Fortress of Heptapyrgion, may require a ticket for entry, with prices typically ranging from €2 to €6 depending on the site. The walls themselves can be explored freely, with several sections offering excellent opportunities for photos and a better understanding of Thessaloniki's defensive history.

A visit to the Byzantine Walls typically takes about 1 to 1.5 hours, but it can be extended if you choose to explore the nearby Upper Town, which is filled with traditional houses, Byzantine churches, and excellent viewpoints. The area is perfect for a scenic walk, and the views from the top are breathtaking, allowing you to appreciate Thessaloniki's beauty and history. The Byzantine Walls offer an essential experience for history lovers, providing a tangible connection to the past and the city's enduring heritage.

9. Church of Agios Dimitrios

The Church of Agios Dimitrios is one of Thessaloniki's most important and revered landmarks, dedicated to the city's patron saint, Saint Dimitrios. This stunning Byzantine church, dating back to the 7th century, is renowned for its architectural beauty, historical significance, and religious importance. Agios Dimitrios is famous not only for its exquisite mosaics and frescoes but also for its role in the city's Christian history. The church was built over the site where Saint Dimitrios, the patron saint of Thessaloniki, was martyred and buried. It remains a major pilgrimage destination for Orthodox Christians from around the world. In addition to its religious significance, the church houses a crypt where visitors can view the saint's relics.

Getting to the Church of Agios Dimitrios is straightforward, as it is located in the heart of Thessaloniki's historic center. It is just a short walk from Aristotelous Square and other popular landmarks, such as the Roman Forum and the White Tower. Public buses and taxis also frequently pass through the area, making the church easy to access from different parts of the city. Its central location makes it a perfect addition to any sightseeing itinerary in Thessaloniki.

The church is open to the public daily, with visiting hours typically from 7:00 AM to 9:00 PM, although these hours may vary slightly during religious holidays. Admission to the Church of Agios Dimitrios is free, but donations are welcome, and there is a small fee for visiting the crypt and the adjoining archaeological site. The entrance to the crypt is located at the lower level of the church and contains several relics, including those of Saint Dimitrios, which are of great historical and spiritual importance.

A visit to the church typically takes around 30 minutes to an hour, depending on how much time you wish to spend exploring the crypt and admiring the church's interior. The stunning mosaics, which cover the walls and ceiling, as well as the beautiful marble floors and intricate iconography, make for an awe-inspiring experience. Whether you are visiting for religious reasons or simply to admire the architecture and history, the Church of Agios Dimitrios offers a deeply enriching experience.

10. Archaeological Museum of Thessaloniki

The Archaeological Museum of Thessaloniki is one of the city's most significant cultural institutions, offering an in-depth look at the rich history of Thessaloniki and its surrounding regions. The museum showcases artifacts from various periods of Greek history, from prehistoric times to the Roman and Byzantine eras. Its extensive collection includes ancient pottery, sculptures, coins, mosaics, and everyday objects that illuminate the daily lives of the people who lived in this historically important area. One of the museum's most notable exhibits is the collection of Roman-era artifacts, which reflect Thessaloniki's prominence as a major Roman city. The museum is also home to impressive finds from nearby archaeological sites, such as the ancient city of Vergina, which is famous for the tomb of King Philip II, the father of Alexander the Great.

The Archaeological Museum of Thessaloniki is located in the city center, making it easy to access from other major attractions. It is situated near the White Tower and the waterfront, just a short walk from the city's main square, Aristotelous Square. The museum is also well-served by public transportation, with several bus stops nearby, and taxis are an easy way to reach the location if you prefer not to walk.

The museum is open every day except Monday, typically from 8:00 AM to 8:00 PM. Admission to the museum costs around €8 for adults, with reduced fees for students and seniors. Admission is free on certain days of the year, such as International Museum Day, so it's worth checking the museum's website for any special offers or free entry days. There is also a small shop at the museum where you can purchase books, replicas of ancient artifacts, and other souvenirs related to the museum's exhibits.

A visit to the Archaeological Museum of Thessaloniki usually takes around 1 to 2 hours, depending on how much time you wish to spend exploring the exhibits. The museum offers informative descriptions in both Greek and English, and audio guides are available for those who wish to learn more about the artifacts. The museum is a must-see for history enthusiasts, offering a fascinating glimpse into the ancient past of Thessaloniki and its role in Greek and Roman history. Whether you're a casual visitor or a history lover, the museum provides an enriching experience that deepens your understanding of Thessaloniki's heritage.

11. Museum of Byzantine Culture

The Museum of Byzantine Culture in Thessaloniki is one of Greece's premier cultural institutions, dedicated to preserving and showcasing the region's rich Byzantine heritage. Opened in 2002, the museum houses a remarkable collection of artifacts from the Byzantine Empire, spanning from the 3rd to the 15th century. Visitors can explore a variety of exhibits, including exquisite mosaics, frescoes, ceramics, jewelry, coins, and religious icons, all of which offer insight into the cultural and religious life during the Byzantine era. The museum's modern design allows for a seamless integration of historical displays with cutting-edge exhibition techniques, making it a must-visit for anyone interested in Byzantine history and art.

The Museum of Byzantine Culture is conveniently located near the Thessaloniki Archaeological Museum, making it an easy addition to your cultural tour of the city. It is situated just a short walk from the waterfront and is well-connected by public transport, with several bus lines stopping nearby. If you are coming from the city center, the museum can be easily reached on foot, as it is only about 15 minutes away from Aristotelous Square. Taxis are also an option for those who prefer a quicker, more comfortable journey.

The museum is open every day except Mondays, with typical hours from 8:00 AM to 8:00 PM. Admission to the museum costs around €8 for adults, with reduced rates for students, seniors, and groups. There are also family tickets available. The museum occasionally offers free entry during special events or days, so be sure to check for any discounts or free admission days. Inside, you'll find a well-stocked gift shop offering books, replicas of artifacts, and other souvenirs related to Byzantine culture.

A visit to the Museum of Byzantine Culture typically takes about 1 to 2 hours, depending on your interest in the exhibits. For those wishing to delve deeper into the displays, audio guides are available in multiple languages, providing informative commentary on the collection. The museum is an essential stop for history enthusiasts, offering a comprehensive overview of Byzantine culture and its lasting influence on the world. Whether you are fascinated by religious iconography, architecture, or Byzantine artifacts, this museum offers a rich, educational experience for all visitors.

.

12. Thessaloniki Science Center and Technology Museum (NOESIS)

The Thessaloniki Science Center and Technology Museum, also known as NOESIS, is one of the city's most engaging and interactive museums, offering an exciting experience for visitors of all ages. Located on the outskirts of the city, NOESIS is dedicated to science, technology, and innovation, with exhibits that explore a wide range of topics, from physics and astronomy to robotics and engineering. The museum is divided into several sections, including hands-on exhibits, educational workshops, and a planetarium, providing an immersive experience for anyone interested in the world of science. The planetarium, one of the largest in Greece, offers stunning shows on space exploration, the solar system, and the universe, making it a highlight of the visit. The museum also features an impressive collection of vintage cars, as well as interactive displays that allow visitors to engage with technology in a fun and educational way.

Getting to NOESIS is straightforward, though it is located a bit further from the city center. It can be reached by car in about 20 minutes from Aristotelous Square, with ample parking available at the museum. Alternatively, public buses serve the area, and there are taxi services for those who prefer more convenience. The museum is easily accessible from most parts of Thessaloniki, making it a great option for a day trip from the city center.

The museum is open daily, except for certain public holidays, from 10:00 AM to 5:00 PM. Admission prices typically range from €6 to €8 for adults, with reduced rates for students and children. Tickets for the planetarium shows are sold separately, with prices ranging from €4 to €5 per person, depending on the show. The museum offers a variety of educational programs and workshops for school groups and families, making it an excellent choice for those traveling with children.

A visit to NOESIS can take anywhere from 1.5 to 3 hours, depending on how long you wish to explore the exhibits and attend any planetarium shows. The museum is designed to be both informative and entertaining, with plenty of interactive elements that encourage learning through play. Whether you are a science enthusiast, a family looking for a fun day out, or simply curious about the wonders of technology, NOESIS offers a fascinating and enjoyable experience that is sure to leave a lasting impression.

13. Modiano Market

Modiano Market is one of Thessaloniki's most vibrant and historic landmarks, offering visitors a chance to experience the city's rich cultural diversity and bustling marketplace atmosphere. Built in 1922, this covered market is a testament to the city's heritage, combining a mix of traditional and modern elements. The market is named after its architect, Eli Modiano, and is located in the heart of the city, near Aristotelous Square. It is a place where local vendors sell fresh produce, meats, fish, cheeses, spices, and a wide variety of other goods. Visitors can also find specialty shops offering traditional Greek products, such as olives, honey, and handmade goods. Modiano Market is also home to small eateries serving authentic Greek street food, making it a great spot to enjoy local delicacies while soaking in the lively atmosphere.

Getting to Modiano Market is easy, as it is centrally located in Thessaloniki, within walking distance from key landmarks like the White Tower and the Archaeological Museum. The market is accessible by public transportation, with bus stops nearby, and taxis can drop you off right at the entrance. If you prefer walking, it's only a 10-minute stroll from Aristotelous Square, which is the main hub of the city.

There is no entrance fee to visit Modiano Market, as it is an open public market. However, it's advisable to bring cash if you plan to purchase anything, as some of the smaller vendors may not accept card payments. The market is open every day except Sundays, with operating hours typically from 7:00 AM to 3:00 PM. On Saturdays, the market can get especially busy, as locals come to shop for the weekend.

A visit to Modiano Market can take anywhere from 30 minutes to 1.5 hours, depending on how much time you wish to spend exploring the stalls, tasting local products, and chatting with the vendors. The market is a great place to experience the city's authentic atmosphere and witness the daily life of Thessaloniki's residents. Whether you're a foodie looking for fresh ingredients, a shopper interested in traditional goods, or simply want to enjoy the lively ambiance, Modiano Market is a must-see destination. It offers a genuine taste of Thessaloniki's local culture and is a perfect spot to immerse yourself in the city's unique charm.

12. Kapani Market

Kapani Market, also known as the Modiano's younger counterpart, is one of Thessaloniki's oldest and most famous open-air markets. Located in the heart of the city, this vibrant market offers visitors an authentic slice of everyday life in Thessaloniki, showcasing a rich variety of local products and goods. The market is a maze of narrow alleys filled with a diverse range of stalls selling fresh produce, meat, fish, spices, herbs, traditional Greek cheeses, olives, and baked goods. Kapani is especially renowned for its colorful and fragrant atmosphere, where the local vendors offer a wide selection of regional delicacies, making it an excellent spot for food lovers. The market is also a great place to find traditional Greek textiles, pottery, and handcrafted souvenirs, perfect for those wanting to take home a piece of Thessaloniki's culture.

Kapani Market is centrally located, just a short walk from Aristotelous Square and other major landmarks in the city. It is easily accessible by public transportation, with several bus lines passing nearby, and taxis are also a convenient option. The market is situated in the city's old town area, where visitors can experience the historical and cultural depth of Thessaloniki. It's an ideal stop if you want to immerse yourself in the daily routines of the locals while being close to the city's tourist attractions.

The market is open every day except Sundays, typically from 7:00 AM to 3:00 PM. There is no entrance fee to wander through the market, making it an affordable destination for any traveler. However, visitors should be prepared to carry cash, as many of the smaller vendors may not accept credit cards. The market can get especially busy in the mornings, with locals shopping for fresh produce, so it's a great idea to visit early for the most vibrant experience.

A visit to Kapani Market usually takes around 30 minutes to 1 hour, depending on how much time you want to spend browsing the stalls or sampling the local food. Whether you are looking to buy fresh ingredients, souvenirs, or simply enjoy the lively atmosphere, Kapani Market offers a unique and memorable experience. It's a fantastic way to experience the authentic side of Thessaloniki, away from the typical tourist crowds, and is highly recommended for anyone interested in local culture, food, and history.

15. Ataturk Museum

The Ataturk Museum in Thessaloniki is a historical site dedicated to the life and legacy of Mustafa Kemal Atatürk, the founder of the Republic of Turkey. Located in the city center, the museum occupies the house where Atatürk was born in 1881, and it offers visitors a glimpse into the early life of this influential figure. The museum showcases a range of exhibits related to Atatürk's upbringing, his family, and his later role in shaping modern Turkey.

Items on display include personal artifacts, photographs, documents, and furniture from the house, as well as information about his contributions to Turkish history and politics. Visitors can also learn about the historical context of Thessaloniki during the time of Atatürk's birth, adding depth to the experience.

The museum is located on 1 Vilara Street, not far from Thessaloniki's main shopping streets. It is easily accessible by public transport, with buses regularly passing through the area. From Aristotelous Square, the museum is just a 10-minute walk, making it very convenient for tourists to visit as part of their exploration of the city. The museum's location is also close to other major historical sites in Thessaloniki, so it can be combined with a wider cultural tour of the area.

The Ataturk Museum is open from Tuesday to Sunday, with hours typically from 9:00 AM to 4:00 PM. Admission to the museum is free, making it an affordable cultural experience for all visitors. However, donations are encouraged to help support the museum's maintenance and future exhibitions. The museum does not offer guided tours as standard, but visitors can explore the exhibits at their own pace. Audio guides may be available, but it's a good idea to check in advance or ask upon arrival.

A visit to the Ataturk Museum typically takes between 30 minutes to 1 hour, depending on your level of interest in the exhibits. It's a great place to learn about the historical connection between Thessaloniki and Turkey, offering insights into Atatürk's early life and the political context of the late 19th and early 20th centuries. The museum is a must-visit for history enthusiasts and those interested in the lasting impact of Atatürk on Turkish and world history.

16. Thessaloniki Concert Hall

The Thessaloniki Concert Hall (Megaron Musikis Thessalonikis) is one of the city's premier cultural venues, known for its world-class acoustics and modern architecture. Located in the heart of Thessaloniki, this concert hall hosts a variety of performances, including classical music concerts, theater productions, dance shows, and contemporary music events. With its spacious, elegant design, it is a hub for artistic expression and a significant part of the city's cultural scene.

The concert hall consists of multiple venues, including the impressive M2 Hall, which hosts large-scale performances, and the smaller, more intimate M1 Hall for chamber music and other events. It's also home to the Thessaloniki State Symphony Orchestra, which frequently performs at the venue, offering a rich musical experience to both locals and visitors.

The Thessaloniki Concert Hall is located on the western side of the city, just a short distance from the city center. It can be reached easily by public transport, with bus stops nearby and taxis available for direct access. From Aristotelous Square, the concert hall is about a 10-minute drive, making it an ideal location to visit if you're in the downtown area. For those who prefer to walk, it's about a 20-minute stroll through Thessaloniki's lively streets, offering an opportunity to explore the city on the way.

Ticket prices for performances at the Thessaloniki Concert Hall vary depending on the event. Concert tickets typically range from €10 to €30, with discounts for students, seniors, and groups. Tickets for special performances or international acts may be priced higher. It's advisable to check the event schedule on the concert hall's website ahead of time, as prices and availability can change depending on the performance.

A visit to the Thessaloniki Concert Hall usually lasts from 1.5 to 2 hours, depending on the performance you attend. Before or after a concert, you can enjoy the hall's beautiful surroundings, including a cafe and a small museum dedicated to the history of music in Thessaloniki. Whether you are a lover of classical music or simply looking to experience one of the city's cultural gems, the Thessaloniki Concert Hall offers a memorable and enriching experience for visitors.

17. Heptapyrgion Fortress (Yedi Kule)

Heptapyrgion Fortress, also known as Yedi Kule, is a historic landmark located on the eastern side of Thessaloniki, offering breathtaking views of the city and its surroundings. The fortress was originally built by the Byzantine Empire in the 4th century AD as part of the city's defensive walls. Later, during the Ottoman era, the fortress was expanded and used as a prison. Its name, "Heptapyrgion," meaning "seven towers," refers to the structure's distinctive seven towers, which were used for both military defense and as a place of imprisonment. Today, the fortress stands as a symbol of Thessaloniki's rich history, reflecting the city's changing rulers and cultures over the centuries. Visitors can explore the various levels of the fortress, admire its impressive architecture, and enjoy panoramic views of the city and the sea from its elevated position.

The fortress is located on the northern slopes of the city's Acropolis, near the Ano Poli district. It is easily accessible by car or public transport. From the city center, it's about a 10-minute drive, or visitors can take a bus to the nearby stop and walk up to the fortress. If you prefer to walk, it's a 20-25 minute uphill stroll from the city center, allowing you to enjoy the charming streets of the old town along the way.

Admission to the Heptapyrgion Fortress is reasonably priced, with tickets typically costing around €4 for adults. There are discounts for students, seniors, and groups, with tickets usually priced around €2 for these categories. The fortress is open to visitors every day, from 8:00 AM to 3:00 PM, although opening hours may vary during holidays, so it's a good idea to check the schedule in advance.

A visit to the fortress can take between 30 minutes to an hour, depending on how much time you want to spend exploring the towers, walking around the ramparts, and taking in the views. While at the site, you can also visit the small museum housed within the fortress, which showcases historical artifacts related to its use throughout the centuries. Heptapyrgion Fortress is a must-visit for history buffs and anyone interested in experiencing the medieval charm of Thessaloniki while enjoying one of the city's most scenic viewpoints.

18. Thessaloniki International Fair (TIF)

The Thessaloniki International Fair (TIF) Area is one of the most important cultural and business landmarks in the city, hosting the annual Thessaloniki International Fair, which has been taking place since 1926. This massive exhibition complex serves as the main venue for the fair, attracting businesses, exhibitors, and visitors from all over the world. The TIF is a dynamic space that brings together a wide array of industries, including technology, fashion, art, and gastronomy. Throughout the year, the fairgrounds also host various events, including concerts, trade shows, and conferences, making it a vital cultural and economic hub for Thessaloniki. During the TIF event itself, the area comes alive with thousands of visitors exploring the diverse exhibitions, engaging with innovative products, and experiencing the lively atmosphere. The fair also features performances and local food vendors, providing an all-encompassing cultural experience.

The TIF Area is centrally located in Thessaloniki, within walking distance from the city center and close to major landmarks like the White Tower. The venue is easily accessible by public transportation, including buses and taxis. If you're staying in the city center, it's only a 10-minute walk to reach the fairgrounds, allowing visitors to enjoy the surrounding streets and architecture along the way.

During the Thessaloniki International Fair, ticket prices vary depending on the event and the specific days you plan to attend. Entry for adults typically costs between €5 and €10, with discounts available for students, seniors, and groups. For some special events, like concerts or international performances, additional ticketing may be required, and prices can vary. It's recommended to check the TIF website for up-to-date information on ticket prices and schedules before your visit.

While the fair itself runs for about a week in September, the venue is open throughout the year for various exhibitions and events, and visiting can take anywhere from 1 hour to several hours, depending on the events you wish to attend. The TIF Area is a perfect destination for those interested in commerce, culture, and modern innovations, providing a unique opportunity to engage with the latest trends in a dynamic and energetic environment. Whether you're attending the fair or visiting during an off-peak time, the TIF Area offers a memorable and enriching experience for any traveler.

19. Kalamaria Beach and Marina

Kalamaria Beach and Marina, located in the Kalamaria district of Thessaloniki, offers a perfect blend of natural beauty, relaxation, and vibrant activity. The beach stretches along the waterfront, providing visitors with stunning views of the Aegean Sea and the nearby coastline. Known for its calm waters and clean sand, it's an ideal spot for sunbathing, swimming, and enjoying the Mediterranean climate. The marina area adds to the charm, with yachts and boats lining the shore, creating a picturesque setting for a leisurely walk or a quiet afternoon. The area around Kalamaria Beach and Marina also features numerous cafes, restaurants, and shops, making it a popular destination for both locals and tourists. Whether you're looking to relax by the sea, enjoy water activities, or explore the surrounding eateries and shops, Kalamaria offers a laid-back atmosphere combined with the beauty of Thessaloniki's coastal charm.

Kalamaria Beach is easily accessible from the city center of Thessaloniki, located approximately 6 kilometers southeast. It can be reached by taxi in around 15 minutes, or visitors can take a bus from various points in the city. Bus routes regularly connect the city center to Kalamaria, and the local transportation network makes getting to the beach quite convenient. If you prefer walking, it's about a 45-minute stroll along the seafront, offering beautiful views of the bay as you head toward the beach.

There is no entrance fee for Kalamaria Beach, making it a budget-friendly destination for travelers. Visitors can enjoy the beach and the surrounding area at no cost, though there may be charges for renting beach chairs or umbrellas, depending on the establishment you choose to relax at. Some restaurants and cafes may require a minimum spend if you plan to sit by the sea.

A visit to Kalamaria Beach can last anywhere from an hour to several hours, depending on your activities. If you enjoy swimming, walking along the marina, or trying out local seafood at one of the nearby restaurants, you could easily spend a half-day or more in the area. The marina also offers opportunities for boat rentals, allowing visitors to explore the coastline from the water. Kalamaria Beach and Marina is an excellent choice for those seeking a peaceful escape by the sea while still being close to the city's vibrant atmosphere.

20. Jewish Museum of Thessaloniki

The Jewish Museum of Thessaloniki is a key cultural and historical landmark, offering a deep insight into the rich Jewish heritage of the city. Established in 2001, the museum is housed in a beautiful building that once served as the residence of a prominent Jewish family. The museum chronicles the history of the Jewish community in Thessaloniki, which dates back to Roman times and flourished during the Ottoman Empire. The exhibits highlight the community's contributions to the city, as well as the challenges they faced, particularly during World War II, when many Jews from Thessaloniki were deported to concentration camps. The museum showcases various artifacts, documents, photographs, and personal stories that provide a poignant and informative look at the Jewish experience in Thessaloniki. Visitors can explore the exhibitions that detail the life of Jewish families in the city, their traditions, religious practices, and the tragic losses they suffered during the Holocaust.

The museum is centrally located, close to the city's center, making it easily accessible by foot, taxi, or public transport. If you are staying in the city center, it's just a 10-minute walk to the museum, and it is situated near other important landmarks, such as the White Tower and the Ladadika district. The Jewish Museum of Thessaloniki is located at Agiou Mina 13, and there are several bus routes that pass nearby, making it convenient to visit even if you're not within walking distance.

The museum charges an admission fee of approximately €4 for adults, with discounts for students, seniors, and groups. There is also a reduced rate of around €2 for these categories. The museum is open daily except for major holidays, with opening hours from 9:30 AM to 5:00 PM. Visitors should allocate about 1 to 1.5 hours to fully explore the exhibits, as the museum offers a detailed and immersive experience. There are guided tours available for an additional fee, providing an in-depth understanding of the exhibits and the history of the Jewish community in Thessaloniki.

The Jewish Museum of Thessaloniki is an essential stop for anyone interested in the city's diverse cultural history, offering an educational and moving experience. Whether you are fascinated by the history of the Jewish people in Greece or want to learn more about Thessaloniki's past, the museum provides a thoughtful and informative perspective on the city's multicultural identity.

21. Pasha's Gardens

Pasha's Gardens (Kipos tou Pascha) is a serene and historical park located in the heart of Thessaloniki, offering a peaceful retreat amidst the bustling city. This lush garden dates back to the Ottoman era and was originally part of the residence of the Pasha, the regional governor of Thessaloniki. Today, it serves as a public park where visitors can enjoy a relaxing environment surrounded by centuries-old trees, manicured lawns, and winding paths.

The park features a variety of plant species, ornamental flowers, and fountains, creating a perfect place to unwind, take a leisurely stroll, or have a picnic. The tranquil atmosphere and historical significance of the gardens make it a hidden gem for those seeking to experience a quieter side of the city. The lush greenery, combined with the remnants of Ottoman-era architecture, provides a glimpse into the past while offering modern amenities for visitors to enjoy.

Located near the city center, Pasha's Gardens are easily accessible by foot, public transport, or taxi. If you're staying in the center of Thessaloniki, it's about a 10-minute walk to the park from major landmarks like the White Tower. It's well-served by bus routes, and taxis can also drop you off directly at the entrance. The gardens are situated close to other attractions, making it a convenient stop if you're exploring the city on foot.

There is no entrance fee to visit Pasha's Gardens, making it an affordable and enjoyable destination for all travelers. It's a public park, open year-round, and visitors are free to explore the grounds at their leisure. Although there is no formal admission charge, there may be occasional events or exhibitions that charge a small fee.

A visit to Pasha's Gardens can take anywhere from 30 minutes to 2 hours, depending on how much time you wish to spend relaxing or exploring the park's different areas. It's an ideal spot for those looking to take a break from sightseeing or those interested in photography, as the park's beautiful landscaping offers plenty of scenic views. The peaceful surroundings make it a popular location for both locals and tourists alike to enjoy nature, reflect, and recharge in the heart of Thessaloniki. Whether you're looking to enjoy a calm afternoon or appreciate some local history, Pasha's Gardens provide a memorable and relaxing experience.

When visiting Thessaloniki here are 7 valuable pieces of advice to keep in mind:

1. Public Transportation is Efficient: Thessaloniki has a well-connected public transport system, including buses and taxis, making it easy to get around the city. Consider purchasing a day pass or using the bus network to reach different attractions efficiently.

2. Explore on Foot: Many of Thessaloniki's main attractions are within walking distance of each other, especially in the city center. Strolling through the vibrant streets allows you to fully experience the city's culture, architecture, and local shops.

3. Weather-Appropriate Clothing: Thessaloniki has a Mediterranean climate, so pack accordingly. Summers can be very hot, so light clothing, sunscreen, and a hat are essential. In the winter, the weather is mild, but it's still wise to bring a jacket, as temperatures can drop in the evenings.

4. Embrace the Local Cuisine: Thessaloniki is known for its rich culinary heritage. Don't miss out on tasting local specialties like Bougatsa, Souvlaki, or the iconic Thessaloniki-style Salami. Also, visit traditional markets like Modiano or Kapani for fresh produce and street food.

5. Respect Local Customs: Thessaloniki is a blend of ancient and modern influences, with a strong Greek Orthodox tradition. Be mindful when visiting churches and religious sites; dress modestly, covering your shoulders and knees, and avoid loud behavior.

6. Stay Hydrated: During the hot summer months, the Mediterranean heat can be intense. Carry a water bottle and take frequent breaks in the shade or at one of the many cafes in the city. Thessaloniki has many public fountains, so make use of them to stay refreshed.

7. Plan for Siesta Time: Like many parts of Greece, Thessaloniki's shops and cafes may close for a few hours in the afternoon, typically between 2:00 PM and 5:00 PM, for a siesta. Plan your sightseeing accordingly and take advantage of this time to relax or enjoy a leisurely meal.

Here are 7 of the best services to consider using:

1. Taxi Services: Thessaloniki has a reliable and affordable taxi system. You can easily find a taxi in the city center or book one using various ride-hailing apps, such as Beat or Uber.

2. Thessaloniki Metro: The metro system is in the process of expansion, but parts of it are already functional. It's a convenient and fast way to get around, especially for visiting destinations outside the city center.

3. City Bike Rentals: Thessaloniki is becoming more bike-friendly, and renting a bike is a great way to explore the city at your own pace. Several rental services are available, offering bikes for a few hours or the entire day.

4. Local Tour Guides: Hiring a local guide can enhance your visit by providing deeper insights into Thessaloniki's history and culture. Many guides offer walking tours, focusing on specific areas like Byzantine history or culinary experiences.

5. Delivery Services: Thessaloniki has various food and grocery delivery options, such as e-food and Wolt, making it convenient to enjoy local cuisine or stock up on essentials if you're staying in an apartment.

6. Car Rental Services: If you plan to explore beyond the city, renting a car is a great option. Several rental companies operate in Thessaloniki, giving you the flexibility to visit nearby areas like Mount Olympus or Halkidiki.

7. Concierge Services: Many hotels in Thessaloniki offer concierge services that can assist with booking tickets, arranging airport transfers, and providing personalized recommendations for dining, shopping, and sightseeing.

Top 7 Must-Try Dining Spots in Thessaloniki:

1. Modus: Known for its contemporary Mediterranean cuisine, Modus offers a unique dining experience with creative dishes using fresh local ingredients. Its modern ambiance makes it a favorite for both locals and tourists.

2. Bougatsa Bantis: For a taste of the city's famous pastry, visit Bougatsa Bantis. Here, you can try the traditional bougatsa, a flaky pastry filled with custard, minced meat, or cheese, all served fresh from the oven.

3. Ta Kavouria: This seafood restaurant is a hidden gem in Thessaloniki, offering a variety of fresh seafood dishes in a cozy, rustic setting. The grilled fish and octopus are particularly popular.

4. Ouzeri To Kavouraki: If you're in the mood for traditional Greek meze, this ouzeri offers a wide selection of small plates, including seafood, olives, and grilled vegetables, best enjoyed with a glass of ouzo.

5. La Doze Bar: A trendy spot for casual dining, La Doze Bar serves gourmet burgers, sandwiches, and other comfort food with a twist. It's perfect for a laid-back lunch or dinner in a vibrant neighborhood.

6. Souvlaki Tsiourgas: For an authentic taste of Thessaloniki's iconic street food, head to Souvlaki Tsiourgas. Known for its perfectly grilled souvlaki and pita wraps, it's a must-try for anyone craving Greek fast food.

7. Pantheon: Situated on the top floor of a building, Pantheon offers stunning views of the city alongside a menu filled with traditional Greek and Mediterranean dishes. The restaurant's terrace is especially beautiful during sunset, making it an ideal spot for a romantic dinner.

Here are 7 crucial phone numbers to know:

1. Emergency Services: 112 – This is the general emergency number in Greece for police, fire, or medical emergencies.

2. Police: 100 – For non-emergency police assistance or to report crimes.

3. Ambulance: 166 – In case of a medical emergency, you can contact the ambulance service.

4. Thessaloniki Airport (Macedonia Airport): +30 2310 473 000 – For flight information, inquiries, or assistance at the airport.

5. Thessaloniki Bus Station: +30 2310 595 000 – For information on bus schedules and services departing from the city's central bus station.

6. Taxi Service: 18300 – The main taxi booking number in Thessaloniki, which connects you to reliable taxi services.

7. Tourist Information: +30 2310 236 000 – The official tourist information line to get advice on attractions, events, and general travel assistance in Thessaloniki.

7 unknown facts about Thessaloniki:

1. Thessaloniki was once the capital of the Roman Empire's Eastern part. Known as "Therma," it became an important city under Roman rule, and later, the Byzantine Empire.

2. The city is home to one of the largest Jewish communities in Europe. Thessaloniki was known as the "Jerusalem of the Balkans" before World War II, with a rich Jewish heritage and many historical synagogues.

3. The White Tower, an iconic landmark of Thessaloniki, was originally built as a Byzantine tower but later became part of the Ottoman fortifications. It was used as a prison before being turned into a museum.

4. Thessaloniki's long coastline along the Aegean Sea was once home to a bustling ancient harbor. Despite this, the city has no major beaches in its immediate center today, although nearby Kalamaria offers some popular spots.

5. The city's famous Modiano Market, an architectural gem, was inspired by the markets of Paris. It was designed in the early 20th century and remains a vibrant marketplace today, offering everything from fresh produce to local delicacies.

6. Thessaloniki is the birthplace of many famous historical figures, including the philosopher Aristotle and the renowned musician Vassilis Tsitsanis. The city's cultural and intellectual legacy runs deep.

7. The famous Thessaloniki International Film Festival is one of the oldest and most prestigious film festivals in Europe. Held annually since 1960, it has showcased both international and Greek cinema, helping to elevate the city's cultural standing.

Made in United States
Troutdale, OR
01/06/2025

27632185R20015